Cambridge Young Learners English Tests

Cambridge Starters 3

Examination papers from

University of Cambridge ESOL Examinations:

English for Speakers of Other Languages

CAMBRIDGE
UNIVERSITY PRESS

CAMBRIDGE UNIVERSITY PRESS
Cambridge, New York, Melbourne, Madrid, Cape Town, Singapore, São Paulo

Cambridge University Press
The Edinburgh Building, Cambridge CB2 2RU, UK

www.cambridge.org
Information on this title: www.cambridge.org/9780521755184

First published 2003
6th printing 2006

Printed in Dubai by Oriental Press

A catalogue record for this publication is available from the British Library

ISBN-13 978-0-521-75518-4 Student's Book
ISBN-10 0-521-75518-2 Student's Book

ISBN-13 978-0-521-75519-1 Answer Booklet
ISBN-10 0-521-75519-0 Answer Booklet

ISBN-13 978-0-521-75520-7 Cassette
ISBN-10 0-521-75520-4 Cassette

<u>Contents</u>

Test 1

Test 2

Test 3

Speaking Tests

Contents

Part 1

– 5 questions –

Listen and draw lines. There is one example.

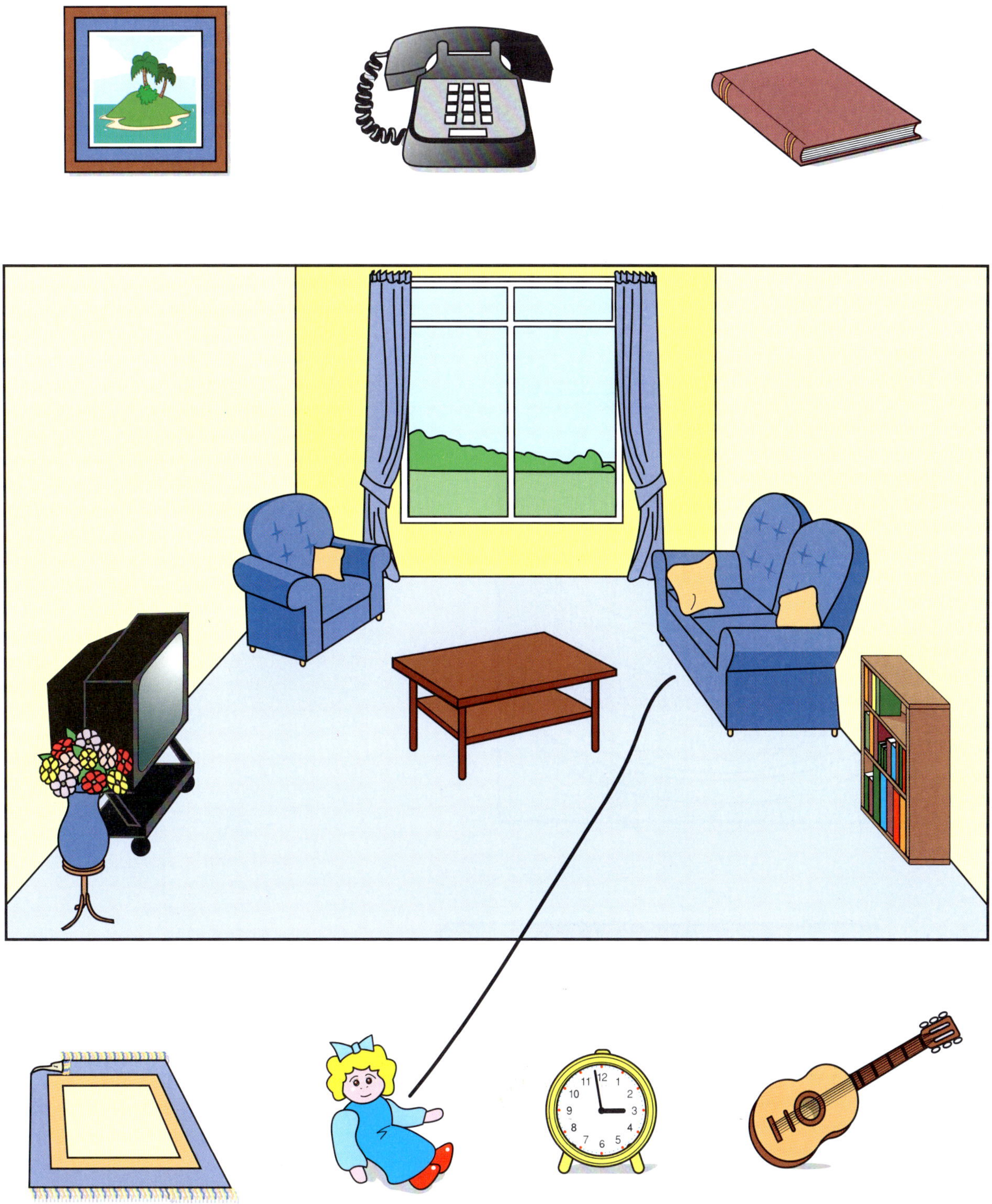

Part 2
– 5 questions –

Listen and write a name or a number.

There are two examples.

.............................Sue.............................

.............................7.............................

1

....

2

Ben ....

3

....

4

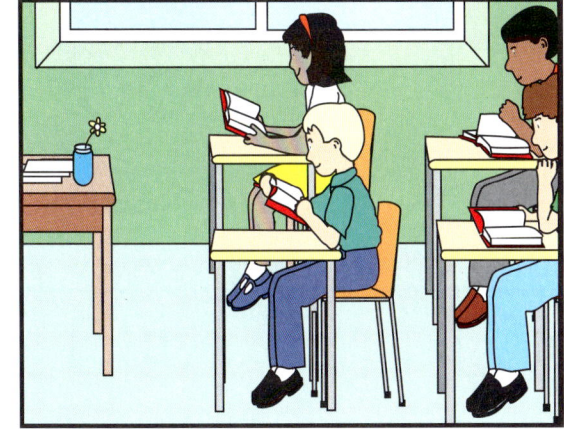

....

5

....

Part 3
– 5 questions –

Listen and tick (✔) the box. There is one example.

What's John drinking?

A ☐   B ✔   C ☐

1   Which boy is Sam?

A ☐   B ☐   C ☐

2   Which is Ann's new dress?

A ☐   B ☐   C ☐

3   Which monster does Sam like?

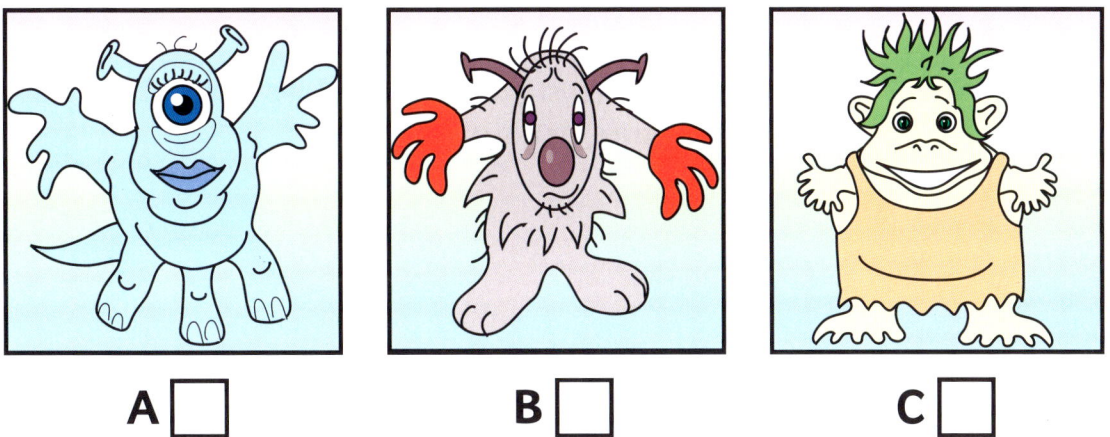

A ☐   B ☐   C ☐

4   How does Bill go to school?

A ☐   B ☐   C ☐

5   What's for supper?

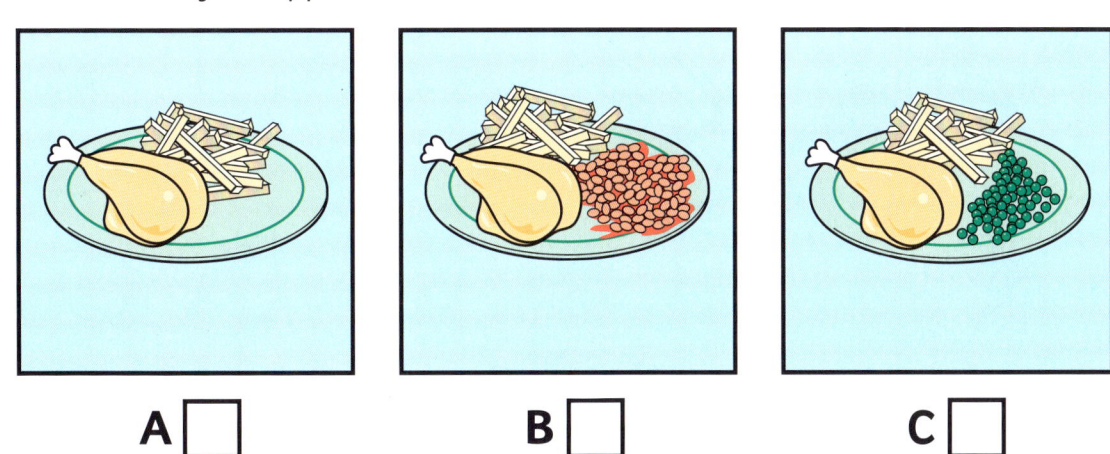

A ☐   B ☐   C ☐

Part 4

– 5 questions –

Listen and colour. There is one example.

Reading and Writing

Part 1
– 5 questions –

Look and read. Put a tick (✔) or a cross (✗) in the box.
There are two examples.

Examples

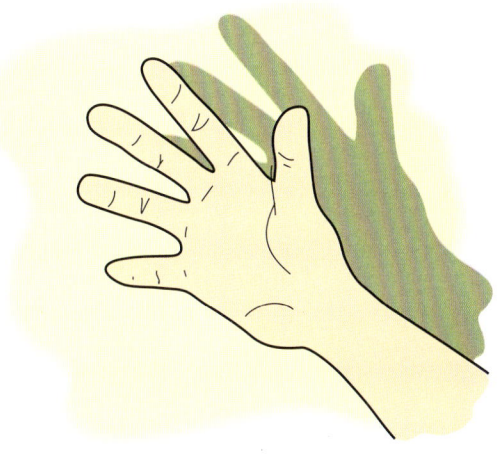

This is a hand.

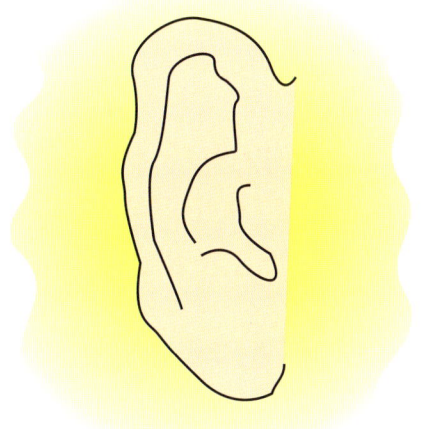

This is an eye.

Questions

1

This is a hippo.

2

This is a bookcase. ☐

3

This is a chicken. ☐

4

This is a chair. ☐

5

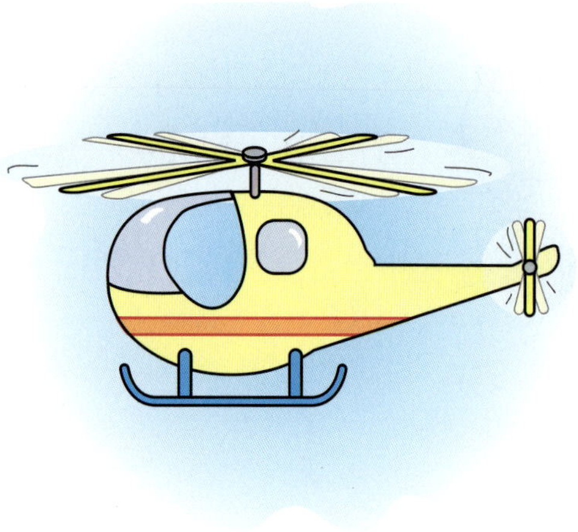

This is a plane. ☐

Part 2
– 5 questions –

Look and read. Write yes or no.

Examples

The boy is wearing a hat. .... *yes*

There are four frogs in the water. .... *no*

Questions

1 The boy's trousers are yellow. ....

2 There is a duck next to the boy. ....

3 The boy is playing with a toy plane. ....

4 There is a bird in the boat. ....

5 The boy's feet are in the water. ....

Part 3
– 5 questions –

Look at the pictures. Look at the letters. Write the words.

Example

<u>d o l l</u>

Questions

1

_ _ _ _

2

_ _ _ _

3

_ _ _ _ _

4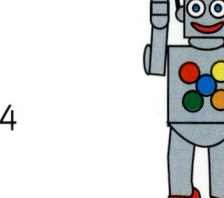

_ _ _ _ _

5

_ _ _ _ _ _

Part 4
– 5 questions –

**Read the story. Look at the pictures and the two examples.
Write one-word answers.**

What am I?

A teacher sits on a ....chair........................... in front of the class.

He puts his ....pens........................... and ruler on me and his

.... under me. The .... stand

next to me and the teacher puts a .... or a cross

on their books. I am like a .... and I am brown.

What am I?

I am a __ __ __ __ .

Part 5
– 5 questions –

Look at the pictures and read the questions. Write one-word answers.

Examples

What is on the table next to the bed?   a .... *lamp*

What is the cat doing?   .... *sleeping*

Questions

1   Which room is Sue in?   her ....

2   Where is Sue now?   in the ....

3   What is Sue eating?   an ....

4   What is the cat drinking?   ....

5   What colour is the sun?   ....

Listening

Part 1
– 5 questions –

Listen and draw lines. There is one example.

Part 2
– 5 questions –

Listen and write a name or a number.

There are two examples.

.... Ann ....

.... 8 ....

1

.... Tree School

2

....

3

....

4

BOAT
COAT
FOAM

....

5

....

Part 3
– 5 questions –

Listen and tick (✔) the box. There is one example.

What's Sue doing?

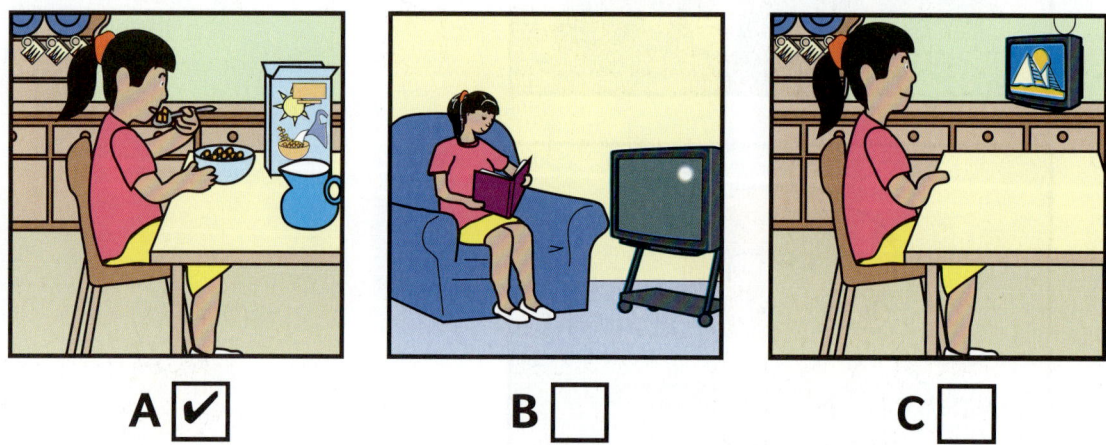

A ✔   B ☐   C ☐

1   What's Tom's favourite animal?

A ☐   B ☐   C ☐

2   Where's the baby?

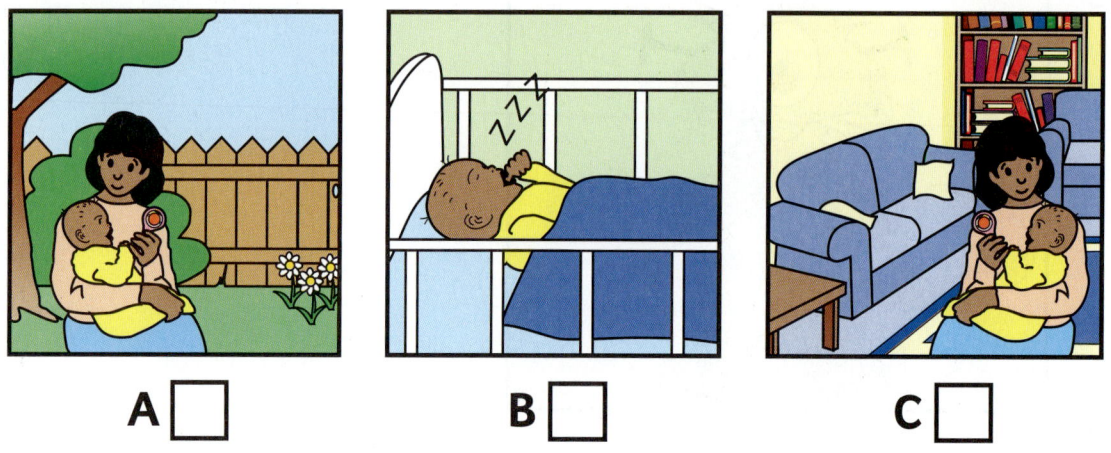

A ☐   B ☐   C ☐

3   What's Ben having for lunch?

A ☐   B ☐   C ☐

4   Which girl is Kim?

A ☐   B ☐   C ☐

5   What does Nick want for his birthday?

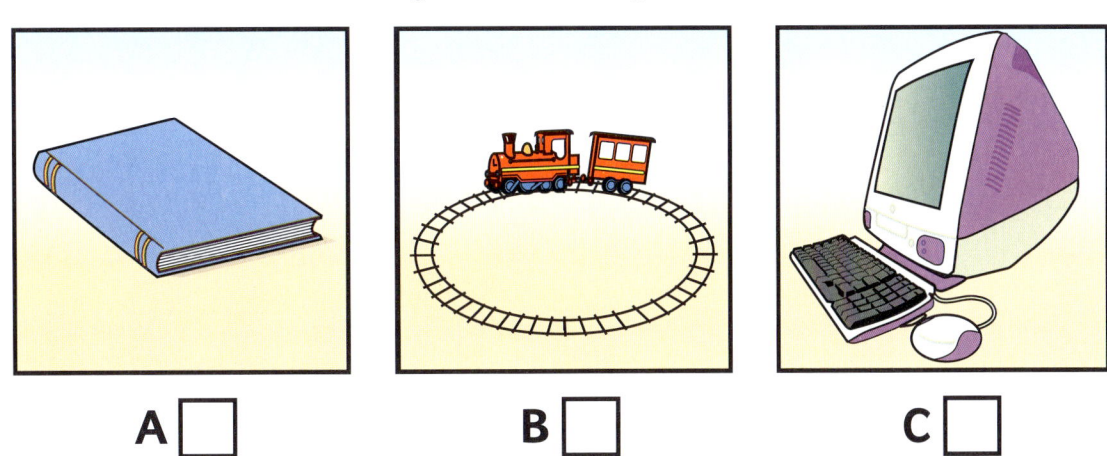

A ☐   B ☐   C ☐

Part 4
– 5 questions –

Listen and colour. There is one example.

Reading and Writing

Part 1
– 5 questions –

Look and read. Put a tick (✔) or a cross (✗) in the box.
There are two examples.

Examples

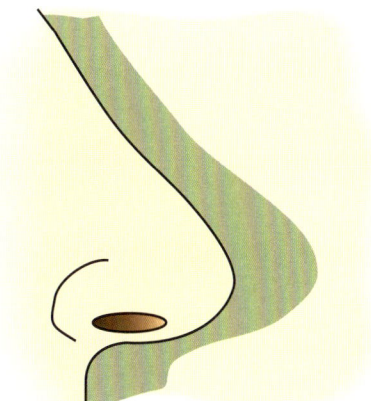

This is a nose.

This is a piano.

Questions

1

This is a wall.

2

This is a kitchen. ☐

3

This is a dress. ☐

4

This is a T-shirt. ☐

5

This is a goat. ☐

Part 2
– 5 questions –

Look and read. Write yes or no.

Examples

There are two cars in the picture. ...... *yes* ......

A man is riding a horse. ...... *no* ......

Questions

1 The man in the red jacket is
   wearing short trousers. ....

2 A girl is bouncing some balls. ....

3 There's a kite in a tree. ....

4 There's a monkey on the motorbike. ....

5 The woman in the blue car is singing. ....

Part 3

– 5 questions –

Look at the pictures. Look at the letters. Write the words.

Example

p i c t u r e

Questions

1  _ _ _ _

2 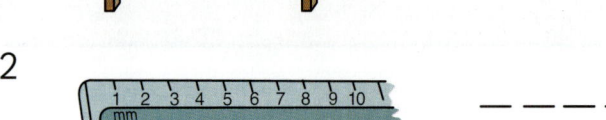 _ _ _ _ _

3 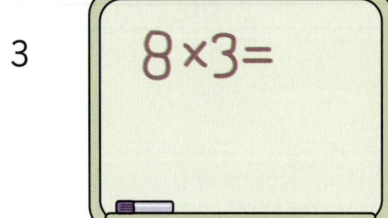 _ _ _ _ _

4 _ _ _ _ _ _

5 _ _ _ _ _ _ _

Part 4
– 5 questions –

**Read the story. Look at the pictures and the two examples.
Write one-word answers.**

What am I?

$$0 \quad \overset{5}{\underset{2}{}} \quad \underset{6}{} \quad 9$$

I have .... numbers .... on me. You can find me in the

.... house .... and in the ....

Some men and women put me in their ....

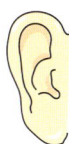

You put part of me next to your .... and part of

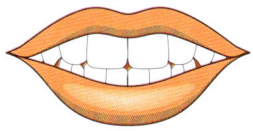

me next to your ....

Then you talk, and your friend can listen to you.

What am I?

I am a __ __ __ __ __ .

Part 5
– 5 questions –

Look at the pictures and read the questions. Write one-word answers.

Examples

What is the girl doing? ....reading..................

Where is the girl's mother? at the ....door..................

Questions

1   Where are the clothes? on the ....

2   Where is the girl putting
    the clothes?   under the ....

3   How many books are there
    in the bookcase?   ....

4   What is the girl eating?   some ....

5   What is the girl's mother picking up?   a ....

Listening

Part 1
– 5 questions –

Listen and draw lines. There is one example.

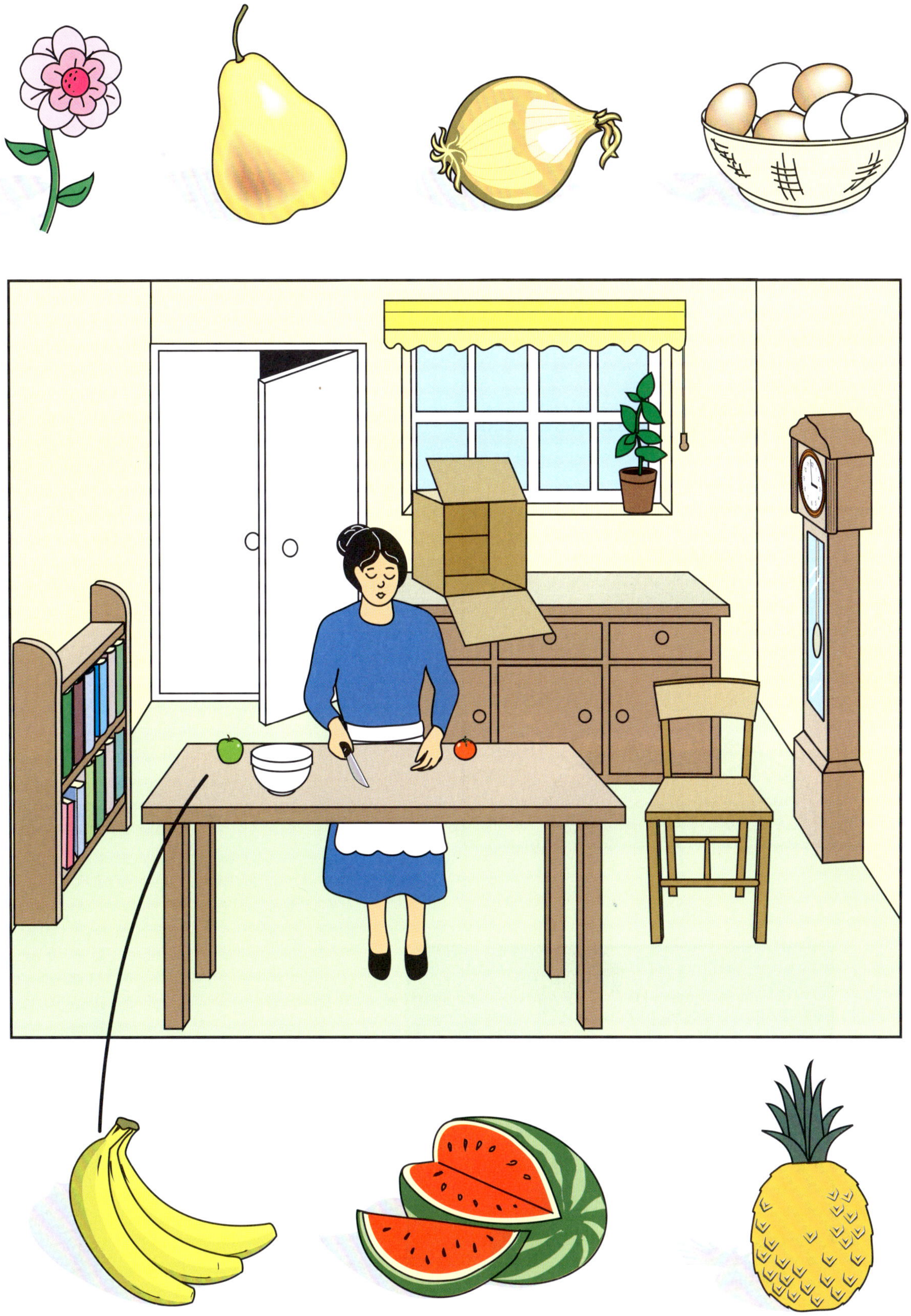

Part 2
– 5 questions –

Listen and write a name or a number.

There are two examples.

.... May

.... 3

1

....

2

..............................Street

3

....

4

Mr ....

5

....

Part 3
– 5 questions –

Listen and tick (✔) the box. There is one example.

What's Pat's favourite food?

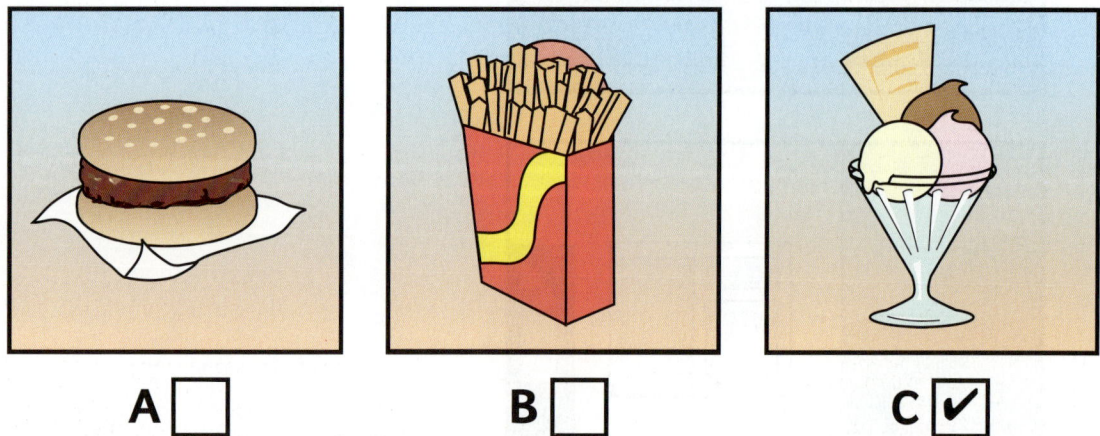

A ☐   B ☐   C ✔

1   Who is Ben's teacher?

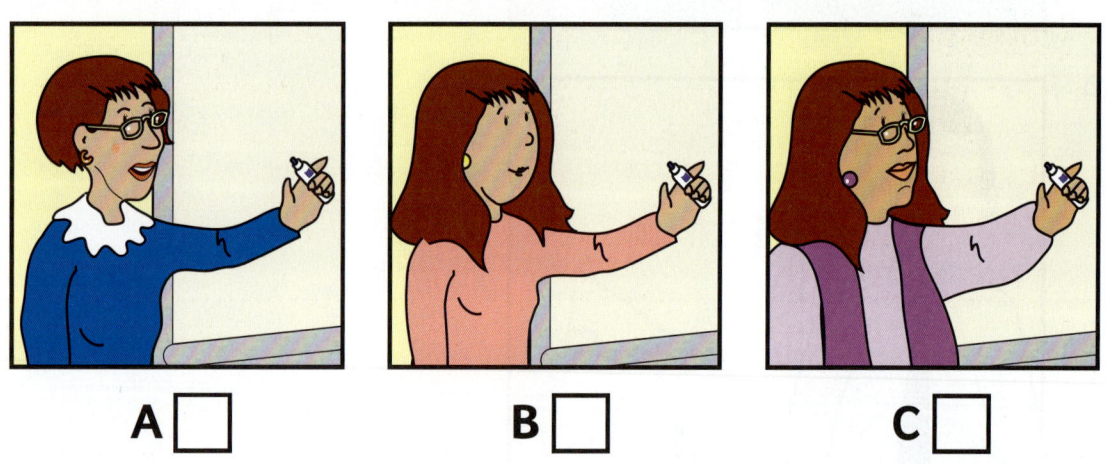

A ☐   B ☐   C ☐

2   Which colour does Mum like?

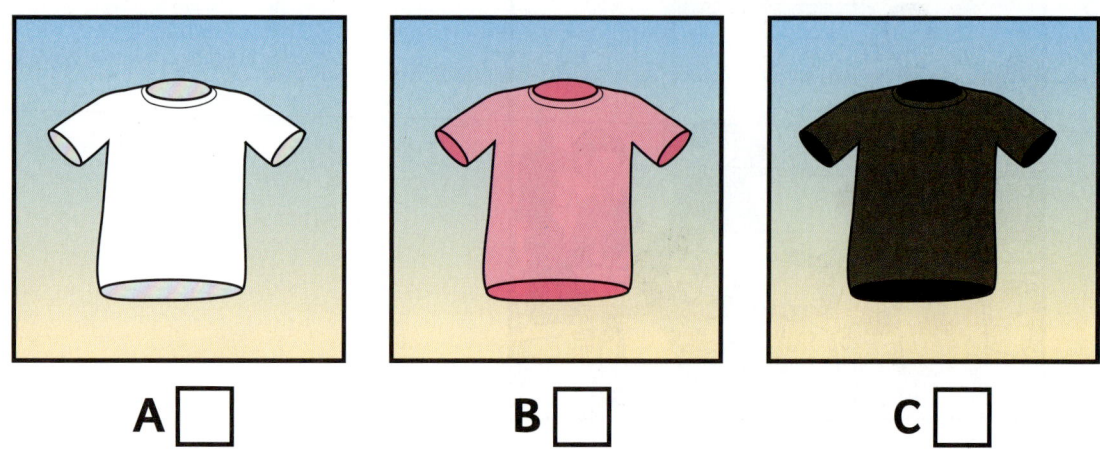

A ☐   B ☐   C ☐

3   Which boy is Tom?

A ☐   B ☐   C ☐

4   Where are Kim's jeans?

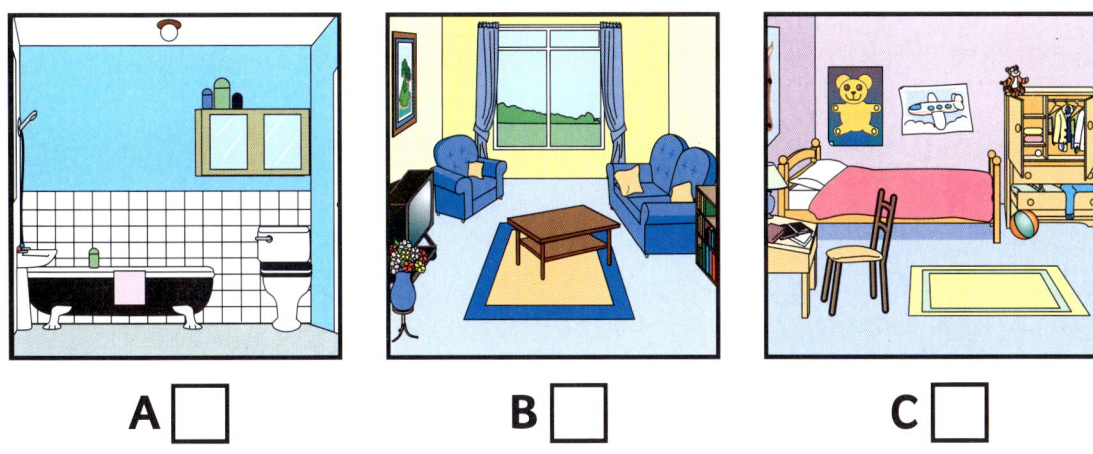

A ☐   B ☐   C ☐

5   What does Bill want for his breakfast?

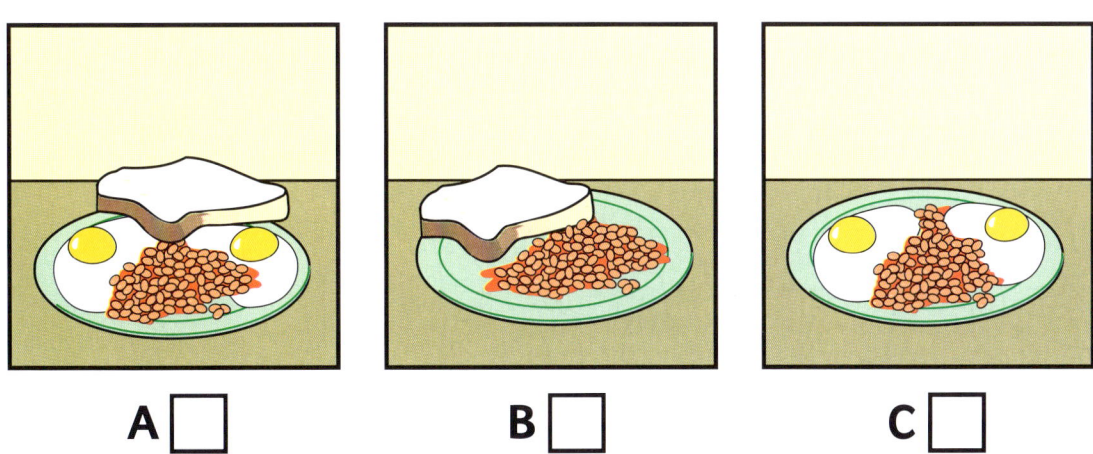

A ☐   B ☐   C ☐

Part 4

– 5 questions –

Listen and colour. There is one example.

Reading and Writing

Part 1
– 5 questions –

**Look and read. Put a tick (✔) or a cross (✗) in the box.
There are two examples.**

Examples

This is a mouse.

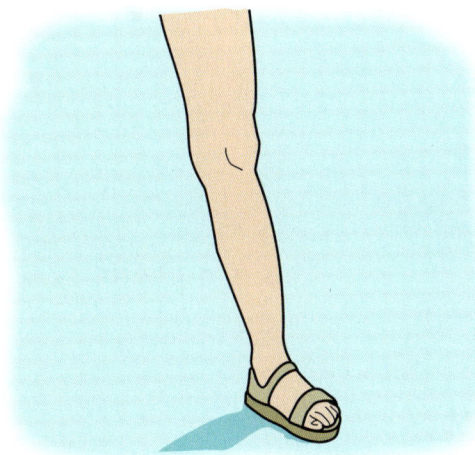

This is an arm.

Questions

1

This is a pear.

2

This is a television.

3

This is a page.

4

This is a photo.

5

This is a shirt.

Part 2
– 5 questions –

Look and read. Write yes or no.

Examples

The man is eating a burger. .... *yes*

The dog has got a sausage. .... *no*

Questions

1 The woman is standing at the window. ....

2 There's a radio under the chair. ....

3 Two children are playing table tennis. ....

4 There are two birds in the big tree. ....

5 The boy is bouncing a ball. ....

Part 3
– 5 questions –

Look at the pictures. Look at the letters. Write the words.

Example

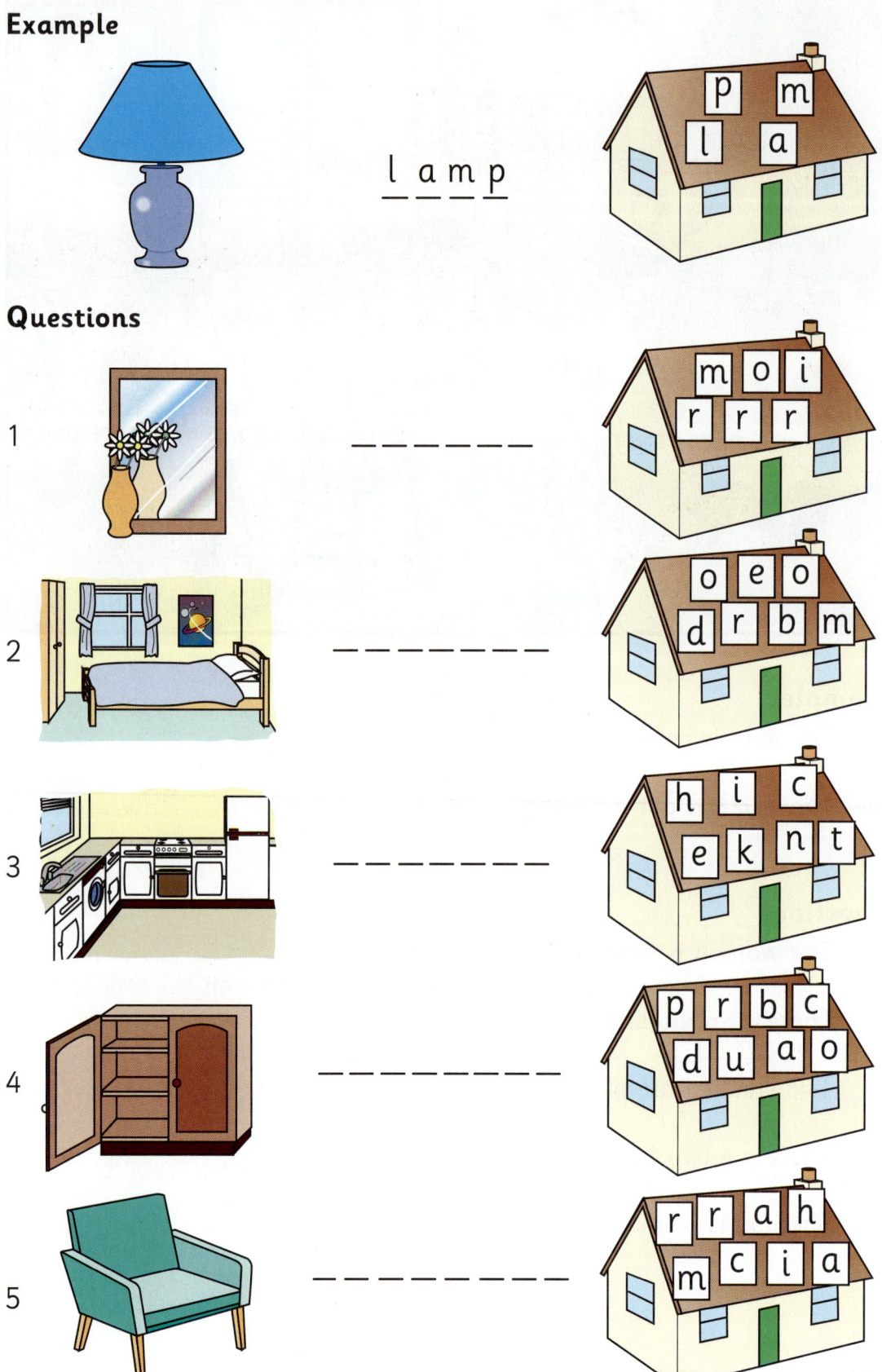

l a m p

Questions

1 _ _ _ _ _ _

2 _ _ _ _ _ _ _

3 _ _ _ _ _ _ _

4 _ _ _ _ _ _ _

5 _ _ _ _ _ _ _

Part 4

– 5 questions –

**Read the story. Look at the pictures and the two examples.
Write one-word answers.**

What am I?

I'm big and boys and .... *girls* .... come to me and sit in my

rooms. In a room there's a .... *clock* .... and there are books

in the .... There are .... on

the walls and the children look at the words and numbers on the

.... There are pens and pencils on the teacher's

.... In my rooms the children have lessons.

What am I?

I am a __ __ __ __ __ __ .

43

Part 5

– 5 questions –

Look at the pictures and read the questions. Write one-word answers.

Examples

What are the children standing
next to?

the ....*shop*..............

What colour is the bus?

...............*yellow*...............

Questions

1   How many children are there
    in the picture?

    ....

2   Who is talking on the phone?   the ....

3   Where are the girls now?   on the ....

4   What has the man got in his hand?   a ....

5   What are the boys pointing at?   some ....

SCENE CARD

OBJECT CARDS

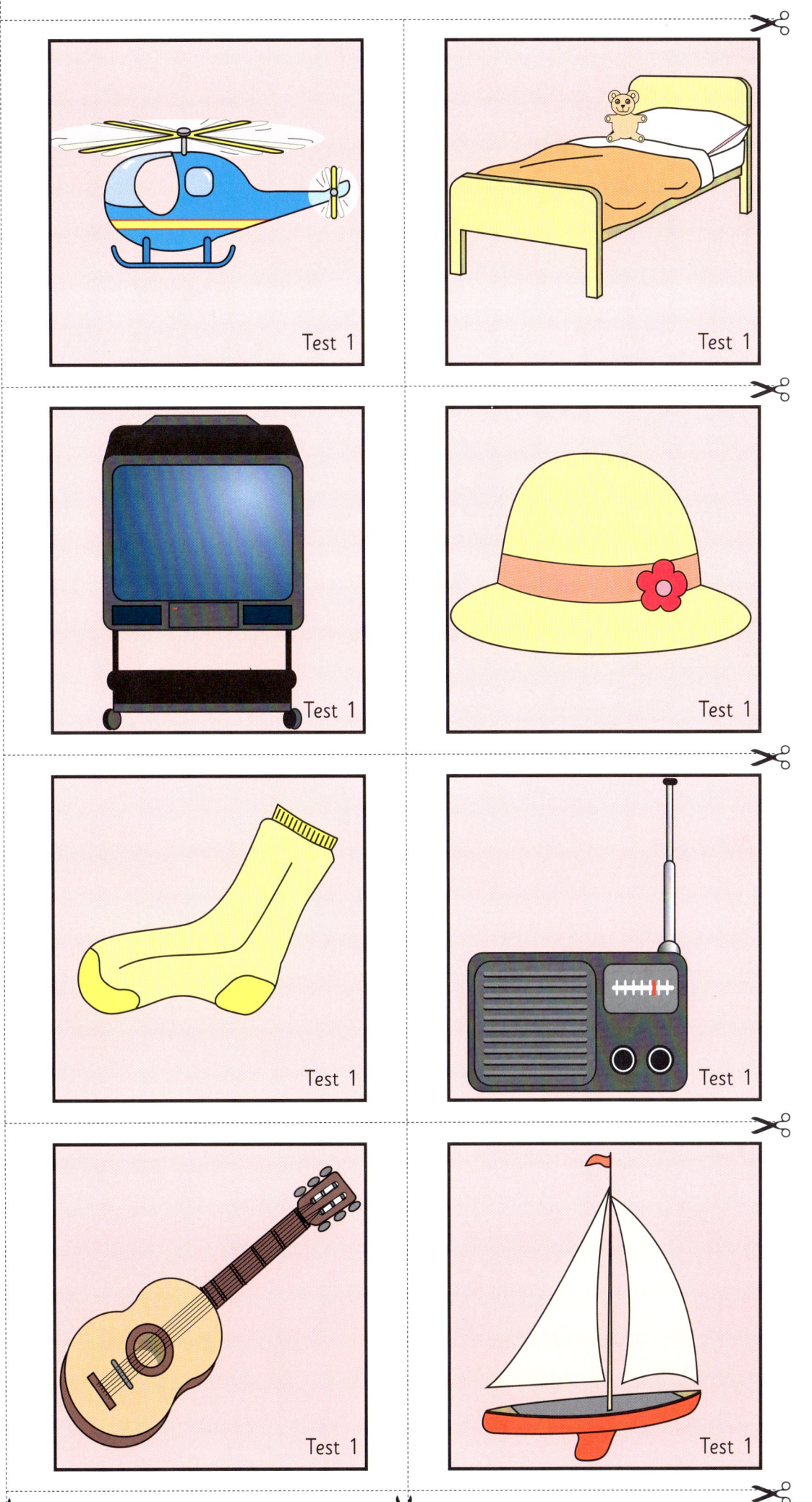

Test 1

Test 1

Test 1

Test 1

Test 1

Test 1

Test 1

Test 1

Speaking

SCENE CARD

Test 2

Test 2

Test 2

Test 2

Test 2

Test 2

Test 2

Test 2

Speaking

SCENE CARD

OBJECT CARDS

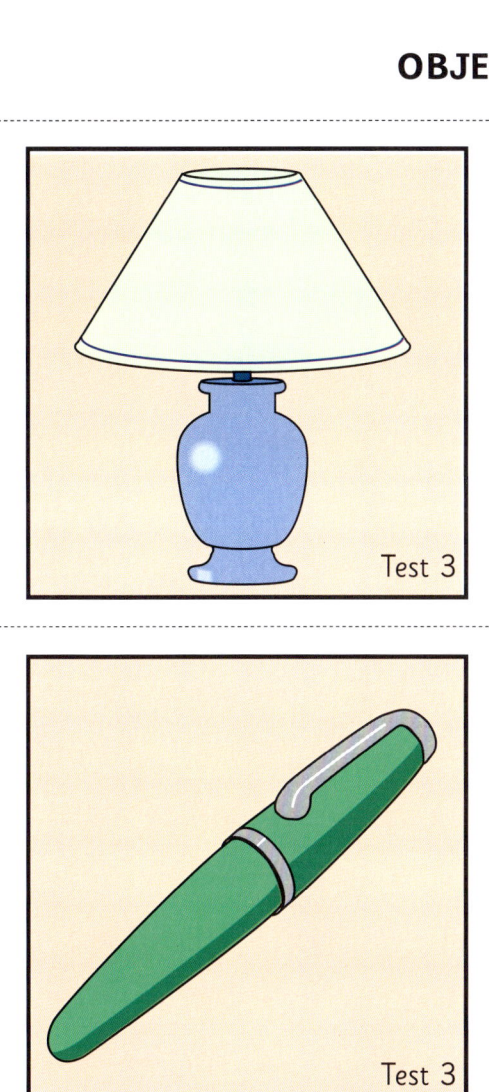

Test 3

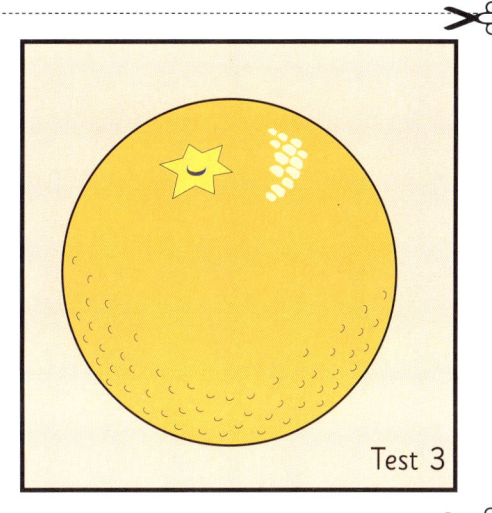

Test 3

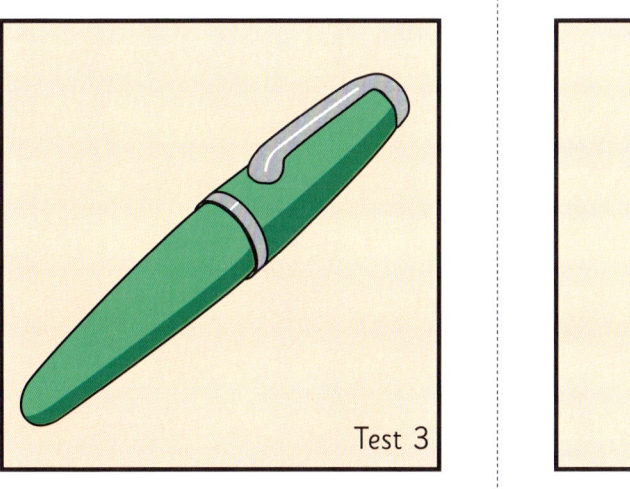

Test 3

Test 3

Test 3

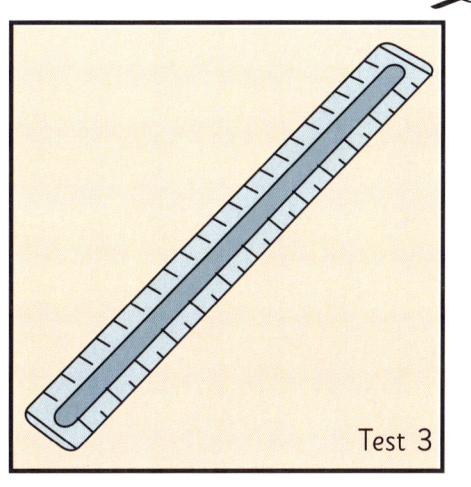

Test 3

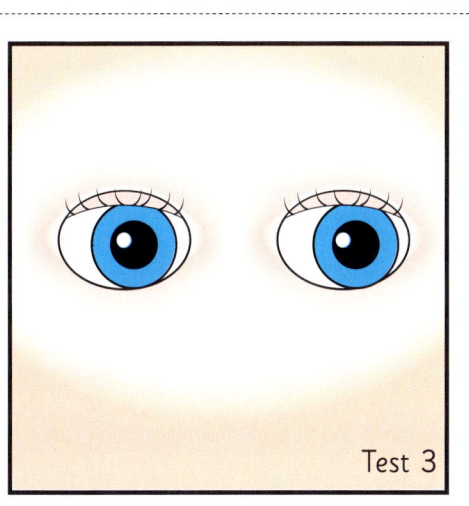

Test 3

Test 3